Home Maintenance Log Book & Planner

This Notebook Belongs To

···

···

···

Home Maintenance Log

MAINTENANCE FOR

DETAILS

DATE ....

PHONE ....

SKETCH DETAIL ....

SYSTEM APLIANCE ....

....

PROBLEM ....

....

....

....

PREPARATION

....

....

....

....

....

....

....

HOW WAS IT RESOLVED?

....

....

....

....

....

....

....

....

....

....

Home Maintenance Log

MAINTENANCE FOR

DETAILS

DATE ....

PHONE ....

SKETCH DETAIL ....

SYSTEM APLIANCE ....

....

PROBLEM ....

....

....

....

PREPARATION

HOW WAS IT RESOLVED?

Home Maintenance Log

MAINTENANCE FOR

DETAILS

DATE ....

PHONE ....

SKETCH DETAIL ....

SYSTEM APLIANCE ....

....

PROBLEM ....

....

....

....

PREPARATION

HOW WAS IT RESOLVED?

Home Maintenance Log

MAINTENANCE FOR

DETAILS

DATE ···

PHONE ···

SKETCH DETAIL ··

SYSTEM APLIANCE ····································

··

PROBLEM ···

··

··

··

PREPARATION

HOW WAS IT RESOLVED?

Home Maintenance Log

MAINTENANCE FOR

DETAILS

DATE ....

PHONE ....

SKETCH DETAIL ....

SYSTEM APLIANCE ....

....

PROBLEM ....

....

....

....

PREPARATION

....
....
....
....
....
....
....

HOW WAS IT RESOLVED?

....
....
....
....
....
....
....
....
....
....

Home Maintenance Log

MAINTENANCE FOR

DETAILS

DATE ....

PHONE ....

SKETCH DETAIL ....

SYSTEM APLIANCE ....

....

PROBLEM ....

....

....

....

PREPARATION

....
....
....
....
....
....
....

HOW WAS IT RESOLVED?

....
....
....
....
....
....
....
....
....
....
....

Home Maintenance Log

MAINTENANCE FOR

DETAILS

DATE ....

PHONE ....

SKETCH DETAIL ....

SYSTEM APLIANCE ....

....

PROBLEM ....

....

....

....

PREPARATION

HOW WAS IT RESOLVED?

Home Maintenance Log

MAINTENANCE FOR

DETAILS

DATE ....

PHONE ....

SKETCH DETAIL ....

SYSTEM APLIANCE ....

....

PROBLEM ....

....

....

....

PREPARATION

HOW WAS IT RESOLVED?

Home Maintenance Log

MAINTENANCE FOR

DETAILS

DATE ....

PHONE ....

SKETCH DETAIL ....

SYSTEM APLIANCE ....
....

PROBLEM ....
....
....
....

PREPARATION

HOW WAS IT RESOLVED?

Home Maintenance Log

MAINTENANCE FOR

DETAILS

DATE ·······································
PHONE ·······································
SKETCH DETAIL ·······························
SYSTEM APLIANCE ····························
···
PROBLEM ····································
···
···
···

PREPARATION

HOW WAS IT RESOLVED?

Home Maintenance Log

MAINTENANCE FOR

DETAILS

DATE ....

PHONE ....

SKETCH DETAIL ....

SYSTEM APLIANCE ....

....

PROBLEM ....

....

....

....

PREPARATION

HOW WAS IT RESOLVED?

Home Maintenance Log

MAINTENANCE FOR

DETAILS

DATE ....

PHONE ....

SKETCH DETAIL ....

SYSTEM APLIANCE ....

....

PROBLEM ....

....

....

....

PREPARATION

HOW WAS IT RESOLVED?

Home Maintenance Log

MAINTENANCE FOR

DETAILS

DATE ....

PHONE ....

SKETCH DETAIL ....

SYSTEM APLIANCE ....

....

PROBLEM ....

....

....

....

PREPARATION

HOW WAS IT RESOLVED?

Home Maintenance Log

MAINTENANCE FOR

DETAILS

DATE ....

PHONE ....

SKETCH DETAIL ....

SYSTEM APLIANCE ....

....

PROBLEM ....

....

....

....

PREPARATION

HOW WAS IT RESOLVED?

Home Maintenance Log

MAINTENANCE FOR

DETAILS

DATE ....

PHONE ....

SKETCH DETAIL ....

SYSTEM APLIANCE ....
....

PROBLEM ....
....
....
....

PREPARATION

HOW WAS IT RESOLVED?

Home Maintenance Log

MAINTENANCE FOR

DETAILS

DATE ....

PHONE ....

SKETCH DETAIL ....

SYSTEM APLIANCE ....
....

PROBLEM ....
....
....
....

PREPARATION

....
....
....
....
....
....
....

HOW WAS IT RESOLVED?

....
....
....
....
....
....
....
....
....

Home Maintenance Log

MAINTENANCE FOR

DETAILS

DATE ....

PHONE ....

SKETCH DETAIL ....

SYSTEM APLIANCE ....
....

PROBLEM ....
....
....
....

PREPARATION

HOW WAS IT RESOLVED?

Home Maintenance Log

MAINTENANCE FOR

DETAILS

DATE ···

PHONE ···

SKETCH DETAIL ··

SYSTEM APLIANCE ···

··

PROBLEM ···

··

··

··

PREPARATION

HOW WAS IT RESOLVED?

Home Maintenance Log

MAINTENANCE FOR

DETAILS

DATE ....

PHONE ....

SKETCH DETAIL ....

SYSTEM APLIANCE ....

....

PROBLEM ....

....

....

....

PREPARATION

HOW WAS IT RESOLVED?

Home Maintenance Log

MAINTENANCE FOR

DETAILS

DATE ···

PHONE ···

SKETCH DETAIL ·······································

SYSTEM APLIANCE ·································

···

PROBLEM ···

···

···

···

PREPARATION

HOW WAS IT RESOLVED?

Home Maintenance Log

MAINTENANCE FOR

DETAILS

DATE ....

PHONE ....

SKETCH DETAIL ....

SYSTEM APLIANCE ....
....

PROBLEM ....
....
....
....

PREPARATION

HOW WAS IT RESOLVED?

Home Maintenance Log

MAINTENANCE FOR

DETAILS

DATE ....

PHONE ....

SKETCH DETAIL ....

SYSTEM APLIANCE ....

....

PROBLEM ....

....

....

....

PREPARATION

....
....
....
....
....
....
....

HOW WAS IT RESOLVED?

....
....
....
....
....
....
....
....
....
....

Home Maintenance Log

MAINTENANCE FOR

DETAILS

DATE ···

PHONE ···

SKETCH DETAIL ···

SYSTEM APLIANCE ···

···

PROBLEM ···

···

···

···

PREPARATION

HOW WAS IT RESOLVED?

Home Maintenance Log

MAINTENANCE FOR

DETAILS

DATE ....

PHONE ....

SKETCH DETAIL ....

SYSTEM APLIANCE ....

....

PROBLEM ....

....

....

....

PREPARATION

HOW WAS IT RESOLVED?

Home Maintenance Log

MAINTENANCE FOR

DETAILS

DATE ....

PHONE ....

SKETCH DETAIL ....

SYSTEM APLIANCE ....

....

PROBLEM ....

....

....

....

PREPARATION

HOW WAS IT RESOLVED?

Home Maintenance Log

MAINTENANCE FOR

DETAILS

DATE ....

PHONE ....

SKETCH DETAIL ....

SYSTEM APLIANCE ....

....

PROBLEM ....

....

....

....

PREPARATION

HOW WAS IT RESOLVED?

Home Maintenance Log

MAINTENANCE FOR

DETAILS

DATE ....

PHONE ....

SKETCH DETAIL ....

SYSTEM APLIANCE ....
....

PROBLEM ....
....
....
....

PREPARATION

HOW WAS IT RESOLVED?

Home Maintenance Log

MAINTENANCE FOR

DETAILS

DATE ....

PHONE ....

SKETCH DETAIL ....

SYSTEM APLIANCE ....

....

PROBLEM ....

....

....

....

PREPARATION

HOW WAS IT RESOLVED?

Home Maintenance Log

MAINTENANCE FOR

DETAILS

DATE ....

PHONE ....

SKETCH DETAIL ....

SYSTEM APLIANCE ....

....

PROBLEM ....

....

....

....

PREPARATION

HOW WAS IT RESOLVED?

Home Maintenance Log

MAINTENANCE FOR

DETAILS

DATE ·
PHONE ·
SKETCH DETAIL ·
SYSTEM APLIANCE ·
· ·
PROBLEM ·
· ·
· ·
· ·

PREPARATION

HOW WAS IT RESOLVED?

Home Maintenance Log

MAINTENANCE FOR

DETAILS

DATE ....

PHONE ....

SKETCH DETAIL ....

SYSTEM APLIANCE ....
....

PROBLEM ....
....
....
....

PREPARATION

HOW WAS IT RESOLVED?

Home Maintenance Log

MAINTENANCE FOR

DETAILS

DATE ··

PHONE ··

SKETCH DETAIL ··

SYSTEM APLIANCE ··

··

PROBLEM ··

··

··

··

PREPARATION

HOW WAS IT RESOLVED?

Home Maintenance Log

MAINTENANCE FOR

DETAILS

DATE ....

PHONE ....

SKETCH DETAIL ....

SYSTEM APLIANCE ....

....

PROBLEM ....

....

....

....

PREPARATION

HOW WAS IT RESOLVED?

Home Maintenance Log

MAINTENANCE FOR

DETAILS

DATE ....

PHONE ....

SKETCH DETAIL ....

SYSTEM APLIANCE ....

....

PROBLEM ....

....

....

....

PREPARATION

HOW WAS IT RESOLVED?

Home Maintenance Log

MAINTENANCE FOR

DETAILS

DATE ···

PHONE ···

SKETCH DETAIL ···

SYSTEM APLIANCE ···
··

PROBLEM ···
··
··
··

PREPARATION

HOW WAS IT RESOLVED?

Home Maintenance Log

MAINTENANCE FOR

DETAILS

DATE ....

PHONE ....

SKETCH DETAIL ....

SYSTEM APLIANCE ....

....

PROBLEM ....

....

....

....

PREPARATION

HOW WAS IT RESOLVED?

Home Maintenance Log

MAINTENANCE FOR

DETAILS

DATE ....

PHONE ....

SKETCH DETAIL ....

SYSTEM APLIANCE ....

....

PROBLEM ....

....

....

....

PREPARATION

HOW WAS IT RESOLVED?

Home Maintenance Log

MAINTENANCE FOR

DETAILS

DATE ·

PHONE ·

SKETCH DETAIL ·

SYSTEM APLIANCE ·

· ·

PROBLEM ·

· ·

· ·

· ·

PREPARATION

HOW WAS IT RESOLVED?

Home Maintenance Log

MAINTENANCE FOR

DETAILS

DATE ....

PHONE ....

SKETCH DETAIL ....

SYSTEM APLIANCE ....

....

PROBLEM ....

....

....

....

PREPARATION

HOW WAS IT RESOLVED?

Home Maintenance Log

MAINTENANCE FOR

DETAILS

DATE ....

PHONE ....

SKETCH DETAIL ....

SYSTEM APLIANCE ....

....

PROBLEM ....

....

....

....

PREPARATION

HOW WAS IT RESOLVED?

Home Maintenance Log

MAINTENANCE FOR

DETAILS

DATE ....

PHONE ....

SKETCH DETAIL ....

SYSTEM APLIANCE ....

....

PROBLEM ....

....

....

....

PREPARATION

HOW WAS IT RESOLVED?

Home Maintenance Log

MAINTENANCE FOR

DETAILS

DATE ··

PHONE ··

SKETCH DETAIL ··

SYSTEM APLIANCE ··
··

PROBLEM ··
··
··
··

PREPARATION

HOW WAS IT RESOLVED?

Home Maintenance Log

MAINTENANCE FOR

DETAILS

DATE ....

PHONE ....

SKETCH DETAIL ....

SYSTEM APLIANCE ....

....

PROBLEM ....

....

....

....

PREPARATION

HOW WAS IT RESOLVED?

Home Maintenance Log

MAINTENANCE FOR

DETAILS

DATE ....
PHONE ....
SKETCH DETAIL ....
SYSTEM APLIANCE ....
....
PROBLEM ....
....
....
....

PREPARATION

HOW WAS IT RESOLVED?

Home Maintenance Log

MAINTENANCE FOR

DETAILS

DATE ....
PHONE ....
SKETCH DETAIL ....
SYSTEM APLIANCE ....
....
PROBLEM ....
....
....
....

PREPARATION

....
....
....
....
....
....
....

HOW WAS IT RESOLVED?

....
....
....
....
....
....
....
....
....
....

Home Maintenance Log

MAINTENANCE FOR

DETAILS

DATE ···

PHONE ···

SKETCH DETAIL ···

SYSTEM APLIANCE ···

···

PROBLEM ···

···

···

···

PREPARATION

···

···

···

···

···

···

···

HOW WAS IT RESOLVED?

···

···

···

···

···

···

···

···

···

···

Home Maintenance Log

MAINTENANCE FOR

DETAILS

DATE ....

PHONE ....

SKETCH DETAIL ....

SYSTEM APLIANCE ....

....

PROBLEM ....

....

....

....

PREPARATION

HOW WAS IT RESOLVED?

Home Maintenance Log

MAINTENANCE FOR

DETAILS

DATE ·····························
PHONE ·····························
SKETCH DETAIL ·····················
SYSTEM APLIANCE ···················
·····································
PROBLEM ··························
·····································
·····································
·····································

PREPARATION

HOW WAS IT RESOLVED?

Home Maintenance Log

MAINTENANCE FOR

DETAILS

DATE ....

PHONE ....

SKETCH DETAIL ....

SYSTEM APLIANCE ....

....

PROBLEM ....

....

....

....

PREPARATION

....

....

....

....

....

....

....

HOW WAS IT RESOLVED?

....

....

....

....

....

....

....

....

....

....

Home Maintenance Log

MAINTENANCE FOR

DETAILS

DATE ···
PHONE ···
SKETCH DETAIL ·································
SYSTEM APLIANCE ·······························
··
PROBLEM ·······································
··
··
··

PREPARATION

HOW WAS IT RESOLVED?

Home Maintenance Log

MAINTENANCE FOR

DETAILS

DATE ....

PHONE ....

SKETCH DETAIL ....

SYSTEM APLIANCE ....

....

PROBLEM ....

....

....

....

PREPARATION

HOW WAS IT RESOLVED?

Home Maintenance Log

MAINTENANCE FOR

DETAILS

DATE ....

PHONE ....

SKETCH DETAIL ....

SYSTEM APLIANCE ....

....

PROBLEM ....

....

....

....

PREPARATION

HOW WAS IT RESOLVED?

Home Maintenance Log

MAINTENANCE FOR

DETAILS

DATE ....

PHONE ....

SKETCH DETAIL ....

SYSTEM APLIANCE ....

....

PROBLEM ....

....

....

....

PREPARATION

HOW WAS IT RESOLVED?

Home Maintenance Log

MAINTENANCE FOR

DETAILS

DATE $\cdots\cdots\cdots\cdots\cdots\cdots\cdots\cdots\cdots\cdots\cdots\cdots$

PHONE $\cdots\cdots\cdots\cdots\cdots\cdots\cdots\cdots\cdots\cdots\cdots$

SKETCH DETAIL $\cdots\cdots\cdots\cdots\cdots\cdots\cdots\cdots$

SYSTEM APLIANCE $\cdots\cdots\cdots\cdots\cdots\cdots\cdots$

$\cdots\cdots\cdots\cdots\cdots\cdots\cdots\cdots\cdots\cdots\cdots\cdots\cdots$

PROBLEM $\cdots\cdots\cdots\cdots\cdots\cdots\cdots\cdots\cdots\cdots$

PREPARATION

HOW WAS IT RESOLVED?

Home Maintenance Log

MAINTENANCE FOR

DETAILS

DATE ....

PHONE ....

SKETCH DETAIL ....

SYSTEM APLIANCE ....
....

PROBLEM ....
....
....
....

PREPARATION

HOW WAS IT RESOLVED?

Home Maintenance Log

MAINTENANCE FOR

DETAILS

DATE ....

PHONE ....

SKETCH DETAIL ....

SYSTEM APLIANCE ....
....

PROBLEM ....
....
....
....

PREPARATION

....
....
....
....
....
....
....

HOW WAS IT RESOLVED?

....
....
....
....
....
....
....
....
....

Home Maintenance Log

MAINTENANCE FOR

DETAILS

DATE ....
PHONE ....
SKETCH DETAIL ....
SYSTEM APLIANCE ....
....
PROBLEM ....
....
....
....

PREPARATION

HOW WAS IT RESOLVED?

Home Maintenance Log

MAINTENANCE FOR

DETAILS

DATE ···

PHONE ··

SKETCH DETAIL ··

SYSTEM APLIANCE ·····································
··

PROBLEM ···
··
··
··

PREPARATION

HOW WAS IT RESOLVED?

Home Maintenance Log

MAINTENANCE FOR

DETAILS

DATE ....

PHONE ....

SKETCH DETAIL ....

SYSTEM APLIANCE ....
....

PROBLEM ....
....
....
....

PREPARATION

HOW WAS IT RESOLVED?

Home Maintenance Log

MAINTENANCE FOR

DETAILS

DATE ....

PHONE ....

SKETCH DETAIL ....

SYSTEM APLIANCE ....
....

PROBLEM ....
....
....
....

PREPARATION

HOW WAS IT RESOLVED?

Home Maintenance Log

MAINTENANCE FOR

DETAILS

DATE ....

PHONE ....

SKETCH DETAIL ....

SYSTEM APLIANCE ....

....

PROBLEM ....

....

....

....

PREPARATION

....

....

....

....

....

....

....

HOW WAS IT RESOLVED?

....

....

....

....

....

....

....

....

....

....

Home Maintenance Log

MAINTENANCE FOR

DETAILS

DATE ···

PHONE ···

SKETCH DETAIL ···

SYSTEM APLIANCE ··

···

PROBLEM ···

···

···

···

PREPARATION

HOW WAS IT RESOLVED?

Home Maintenance Log

MAINTENANCE FOR

DETAILS

DATE ....

PHONE ....

SKETCH DETAIL ....

SYSTEM APLIANCE ....

....

PROBLEM ....

....

....

....

PREPARATION

HOW WAS IT RESOLVED?

Home Maintenance Log

MAINTENANCE FOR

DETAILS

DATE ···

PHONE ···

SKETCH DETAIL ···

SYSTEM APLIANCE ···

···

PROBLEM ···

···

···

···

PREPARATION

HOW WAS IT RESOLVED?

Home Maintenance Log

MAINTENANCE FOR

DETAILS

DATE ....

PHONE ....

SKETCH DETAIL ....

SYSTEM APLIANCE ....
....

PROBLEM ....
....
....
....

PREPARATION

HOW WAS IT RESOLVED?

Home Maintenance Log

MAINTENANCE FOR

DETAILS

DATE ·

PHONE ·

SKETCH DETAIL ·

SYSTEM APLIANCE ·

· ·

PROBLEM ·

· ·

· ·

· ·

PREPARATION

HOW WAS IT RESOLVED?

Home Maintenance Log

MAINTENANCE FOR

DETAILS

DATE ....

PHONE ....

SKETCH DETAIL ....

SYSTEM APLIANCE ....
....

PROBLEM ....
....
....
....

PREPARATION

HOW WAS IT RESOLVED?

Home Maintenance Log

MAINTENANCE FOR

DETAILS

DATE ···

PHONE ···

SKETCH DETAIL ···

SYSTEM APLIANCE ····································

··

PROBLEM ···

··

··

··

PREPARATION

HOW WAS IT RESOLVED?

Home Maintenance Log

MAINTENANCE FOR

DETAILS

DATE ....

PHONE ....

SKETCH DETAIL ....

SYSTEM APLIANCE ....
....

PROBLEM ....
....
....
....

PREPARATION

HOW WAS IT RESOLVED?

Home Maintenance Log

MAINTENANCE FOR

DETAILS

DATE ....

PHONE ....

SKETCH DETAIL ....

SYSTEM APLIANCE ....

....

PROBLEM ....

....

....

....

PREPARATION

HOW WAS IT RESOLVED?

Home Maintenance Log

MAINTENANCE FOR

DETAILS

DATE ....

PHONE ....

SKETCH DETAIL ....

SYSTEM APLIANCE ....
....

PROBLEM ....
....
....
....

PREPARATION

HOW WAS IT RESOLVED?

Home Maintenance Log

MAINTENANCE FOR

DETAILS

DATE ....

PHONE ....

SKETCH DETAIL ....

SYSTEM APLIANCE ....

....

PROBLEM ....

....

....

....

PREPARATION

HOW WAS IT RESOLVED?

Home Maintenance Log

MAINTENANCE FOR

DETAILS

DATE ·······································
PHONE ·······································
SKETCH DETAIL ·······························
SYSTEM APLIANCE ·····························
··
PROBLEM ·····································
··
··
··

PREPARATION

HOW WAS IT RESOLVED?

Home Maintenance Log

MAINTENANCE FOR

DETAILS

DATE ....

PHONE ....

SKETCH DETAIL ....

SYSTEM APLIANCE ....

....

PROBLEM ....

....

....

....

PREPARATION

HOW WAS IT RESOLVED?

Home Maintenance Log

MAINTENANCE FOR

DETAILS

DATE ....

PHONE ....

SKETCH DETAIL ....

SYSTEM APLIANCE ....

....

PROBLEM ....

....

....

....

PREPARATION

HOW WAS IT RESOLVED?

Home Maintenance Log

MAINTENANCE FOR

DETAILS

DATE ....

PHONE ....

SKETCH DETAIL ....

SYSTEM APLIANCE ....

....

PROBLEM ....

....

....

....

PREPARATION

HOW WAS IT RESOLVED?

Home Maintenance Log

MAINTENANCE FOR

DETAILS

DATE ....

PHONE ....

SKETCH DETAIL ....

SYSTEM APLIANCE ....
....

PROBLEM ....
....
....
....

PREPARATION

HOW WAS IT RESOLVED?

Home Maintenance Log

MAINTENANCE FOR

DETAILS

DATE ....

PHONE ....

SKETCH DETAIL ....

SYSTEM APLIANCE ....

....

PROBLEM ....

....

....

....

PREPARATION

HOW WAS IT RESOLVED?

Home Maintenance Log

MAINTENANCE FOR

DETAILS

DATE ....

PHONE ....

SKETCH DETAIL ....

SYSTEM APLIANCE ....

....

PROBLEM ....

....

....

....

PREPARATION

HOW WAS IT RESOLVED?

Home Maintenance Log

MAINTENANCE FOR

DETAILS

DATE ....

PHONE ....

SKETCH DETAIL ....

SYSTEM APLIANCE ....

....

PROBLEM ....

....

....

....

PREPARATION

HOW WAS IT RESOLVED?

Home Maintenance Log

MAINTENANCE FOR

DETAILS

DATE ....
PHONE ....
SKETCH DETAIL ....
SYSTEM APLIANCE ....
....
PROBLEM ....
....
....
....

PREPARATION

HOW WAS IT RESOLVED?

Home Maintenance Log

MAINTENANCE FOR

DETAILS

DATE ··

PHONE ··

SKETCH DETAIL ··

SYSTEM APLIANCE ··

··

PROBLEM ··

··

··

··

PREPARATION

HOW WAS IT RESOLVED?

Home Maintenance Log

MAINTENANCE FOR

DETAILS

DATE ....

PHONE ....

SKETCH DETAIL ....

SYSTEM APLIANCE ....
....

PROBLEM ....
....
....
....

PREPARATION

HOW WAS IT RESOLVED?

Home Maintenance Log

MAINTENANCE FOR

DETAILS

DATE ....

PHONE ....

SKETCH DETAIL ....

SYSTEM APLIANCE ....

....

PROBLEM ....

....

....

....

PREPARATION

HOW WAS IT RESOLVED?

Home Maintenance Log

MAINTENANCE FOR

DETAILS

DATE ....

PHONE ....

SKETCH DETAIL ....

SYSTEM APLIANCE ....
....

PROBLEM ....
....
....
....

PREPARATION

HOW WAS IT RESOLVED?

Home Maintenance Log

MAINTENANCE FOR

DETAILS

DATE ···
PHONE ···
SKETCH DETAIL ·······································
SYSTEM APLIANCE ···································
···
PROBLEM ···
···
···
···

PREPARATION

HOW WAS IT RESOLVED?

Home Maintenance Log

MAINTENANCE FOR

DETAILS

DATE ....

PHONE ....

SKETCH DETAIL ....

SYSTEM APLIANCE ....

....

PROBLEM ....

....

....

....

PREPARATION

HOW WAS IT RESOLVED?

Home Maintenance Log

MAINTENANCE FOR

DETAILS

DATE ···································
PHONE ··································
SKETCH DETAIL ···························
SYSTEM APLIANCE ·························
·····································
PROBLEM ································
·····································
·····································
·····································

PREPARATION

HOW WAS IT RESOLVED?

Home Maintenance Log

MAINTENANCE FOR

DETAILS

DATE ....

PHONE ....

SKETCH DETAIL ....

SYSTEM APLIANCE ....
....

PROBLEM ....
....
....
....

PREPARATION

HOW WAS IT RESOLVED?

Home Maintenance Log

MAINTENANCE FOR

DETAILS

DATE ....

PHONE ....

SKETCH DETAIL ....

SYSTEM APLIANCE ....

....

PROBLEM ....

....

....

....

PREPARATION

HOW WAS IT RESOLVED?

Home Maintenance Log

MAINTENANCE FOR

DETAILS

DATE ·······································

PHONE ·······································

SKETCH DETAIL ·······························

SYSTEM APLIANCE ·····························
···

PROBLEM ·····································
···
···
···

PREPARATION

HOW WAS IT RESOLVED?

Home Maintenance Log

MAINTENANCE FOR

DETAILS

DATE ....

PHONE ....

SKETCH DETAIL ....

SYSTEM APLIANCE ....
....

PROBLEM ....
....
....
....

PREPARATION

HOW WAS IT RESOLVED?

Home Maintenance Log

MAINTENANCE FOR

DETAILS

DATE ....

PHONE ....

SKETCH DETAIL ....

SYSTEM APLIANCE ....

....

PROBLEM ....

....

....

....

PREPARATION

HOW WAS IT RESOLVED?

Home Maintenance Log

MAINTENANCE FOR

DETAILS

DATE ....

PHONE ....

SKETCH DETAIL ....

SYSTEM APLIANCE ....
....

PROBLEM ....
....
....
....

PREPARATION

HOW WAS IT RESOLVED?

Home Maintenance Log

MAINTENANCE FOR

DETAILS

DATE ....

PHONE ....

SKETCH DETAIL ....

SYSTEM APLIANCE ....

....

PROBLEM ....

....

....

....

PREPARATION

HOW WAS IT RESOLVED?

Home Maintenance Log

MAINTENANCE FOR

DETAILS

DATE ···

PHONE ···

SKETCH DETAIL ··

SYSTEM APLIANCE ···
···

PROBLEM ···
···
···
···

PREPARATION

HOW WAS IT RESOLVED?

Home Maintenance Log

MAINTENANCE FOR

DETAILS

DATE ....

PHONE ....

SKETCH DETAIL ....

SYSTEM APLIANCE ....

....

PROBLEM ....

....

....

....

PREPARATION

HOW WAS IT RESOLVED?

Home Maintenance Log

MAINTENANCE FOR

DETAILS

DATE ....

PHONE ....

SKETCH DETAIL ....

SYSTEM APLIANCE ....

....

PROBLEM ....

....

....

....

PREPARATION

HOW WAS IT RESOLVED?

Home Maintenance Log

MAINTENANCE FOR

DETAILS

DATE ....

PHONE ....

SKETCH DETAIL ....

SYSTEM APLIANCE ....
....

PROBLEM ....
....
....
....

PREPARATION

....
....
....
....
....
....
....

HOW WAS IT RESOLVED?

....
....
....
....
....
....
....
....
....

Made in the USA
Coppell, TX
04 May 2022

77397978R00057